Peace

ARISTOPHANES

(Playwright)

[ZHINGOORA BOOKS]

1

This edition is published by
Zhingoora Books.

INTRODUCTION

The 'Peace' was brought out four years after 'The Acharnians' (422 B.C.), when the War had already lasted ten years. The leading motive is the same as in the former play—the intense desire of the less excitable and more moderate-minded citizens for relief from the miseries of war.

Trygaeus, a rustic patriot, finding no help in men, resolves to ascend to heaven to expostulate personally with Zeus for allowing this wretched state of things to continue. With this object he has fed and trained a gigantic dung-beetle, which he mounts, and is carried, like Bellerophon on Pegasus, on an aerial journey. Eventually he reaches Olympus, only to find that the gods have gone elsewhere, and that the heavenly abode is occupied solely by the demon of War, who is busy pounding up the Greek States in a huge mortar. However, his benevolent purpose is not in vain; for learning from Hermes that the goddess Peace has been cast into a pit, where she is kept a fast prisoner, he calls upon the different peoples of Hellas to make a united effort and rescue her, and with their help drags her out and brings her back in triumph to earth. The play concludes with the restoration of the goddess to her ancient honours, the festivities of the rustic population and the nuptials of Trygaeus with Opora (Harvest), handmaiden of Peace, represented as a pretty courtesan.

Such references as there are to Cleon in this play are noteworthy. The great Demagogue was now dead, having fallen in the same action as the rival Spartan general, the renowned Brasidas, before Amphipolis, and whatever Aristophanes says here of his old enemy is conceived in the spirit of 'de mortuis nil nisi bonum.' In one scene Hermes is descanting on the evils which had nearly ruined Athens and declares that 'The Tanner' was the cause of them all. But Trygaeus interrupts him with the words:

"Hold-say not so, good master Hermes; Let the man rest in peace where now he lies. He is no longer of our world, but yours."

Here surely we have a trait of magnanimity on the author's part as admirable in its way as the wit and boldness of his former attacks had been in theirs.

DRAMATIS PERSONAE

TRYGAEUS

TWO SERVANTS OF TRYGAEUS

MAIDENS, DAUGHTERS OF TRYGAEUS

HERMES

WAR

TUMULT

HIEROCLES, a Soothsayer

A SICKLE-MAKER

A CREST-MAKER

A TRUMPET-MAKER

A HELMET-MAKER

A SPEAR-MAKER

SON OF LAMACHUS

SON OF CLEONYMUS

CHORUS OF HUSBANDMEN

SCENE: A farmyard, two slaves busy beside a dungheap; afterwards, in Olympus.

FIRST SERVANT Quick, quick, bring the dung-beetle his cake.

SECOND SERVANT Coming, coming.

FIRST SERVANT Give it to him, and may it kill him!

SECOND SERVANT May he never eat a better.

FIRST SERVANT Now give him this other one kneaded up with ass's dung.

SECOND SERVANT There! I've done that too.

FIRST SERVANT And where's what you gave him just now; surely he can't have devoured it yet!

SECOND SERVANT Indeed he has; he snatched it, rolled it between his feet and bolted it.

FIRST SERVANT Come, hurry up, knead up a lot and knead them stiffly.

SECOND SERVANT Oh, scavengers, help me in the name of the gods, if you do not wish to see me fall down choked.

FIRST SERVANT Come, come, another made from the stool of a young scapegrace catamite. 'Twill be to the beetle's taste; he likes it well ground.

SECOND SERVANT There! I am free at least from suspicion; none will accuse me of tasting what I mix.

FIRST SERVANT Faugh! come, now another! keep on mixing with all your might.

SECOND SERVANT I' faith, no. I can stand this awful cesspool stench no longer, so I bring you the whole ill-smelling gear.

FIRST SERVANT Pitch it down the sewer sooner, and yourself with it.

SECOND SERVANT Maybe, one of you can tell me where I can buy a stopped-up nose, for there is no work more disgusting than to mix food for a beetle and to carry it to him. A pig or a dog will at least pounce upon our excrement without more ado, but this foul wretch affects the disdainful, the spoilt mistress, and won't eat unless I offer him a cake that has been kneaded for an entire day.... But let us open the door a bit ajar without his seeing it. Has he done eating? Come, pluck up courage, cram yourself till you burst! The cursed creature! It wallows in its food! It grips it between its claws like a wrestler clutching his opponent, and with head and feet together rolls up its paste like a rope-maker twisting a hawser. What an indecent, stinking, gluttonous beast! I know not what angry god let this monster loose upon us, but of a certainty it was neither Aphrodite nor the Graces.

FIRST SERVANT Who was it then?

SECOND SERVANT No doubt the Thunderer, Zeus.

FIRST SERVANT But perhaps some spectator, some beardless youth, who thinks himself a sage, will say, "What is this? What does the beetle mean?" And then an Ionian,(1) sitting next him, will add, "I think 'tis an allusion to Cleon, who so shamelessly feeds on filth all by himself."—But now I'm going indoors to fetch the beetle a drink.

f(1) 'Peace' was no doubt produced at the festival of the

Apaturia, which was kept at the end of October, a period

when strangers were numerous in Athens.

SECOND SERVANT As for me, I will explain the matter to you all, children, youths, grownups and old men, aye, even to the decrepit dotards. My master is mad, not as you are, but with another sort of madness, quite a new kind. The livelong day he looks open-mouthed towards heaven and never stops addressing Zeus. "Ah! Zeus," he cries, "what are thy intentions? Lay aside thy besom; do not sweep Greece away!"

7

TRYGAEUS Ah! ah! ah!

SECOND SERVANT Hush, hush! Mehinks I hear his voice!

TRYGAEUS Oh! Zeus, what art thou going to do for our people? Dost thou not see this, that our cities will soon be but empty husks?

SECOND SERVANT As I told you, that is his form of madness. There you have a sample of his follies. When his trouble first began to seize him, he said to himself, "By what means could I go straight to Zeus?" Then he made himself very slender little ladders and so clambered up towards heaven; but he soon came hurtling down again and broke his head. Yesterday, to our misfortune, he went out and brought us back this thoroughbred, but from where I know not, this great beetle, whose groom he has forced me to become. He himself caresses it as though it were a horse, saying, "Oh! my little Pegasus,(1) my noble aerial steed, may your wings soon bear me straight to Zeus!" But what is my master doing? I must stoop down to look through this hole. Oh! great gods! Here! neighbours, run here quick! here is my master flying off mounted on his beetle as if on horseback.

f(1) The winged steed of Perseus—an allusion to a lost

tragedy of Euripides, in which Bellerophon was introduced

riding on Pegasus.

TRYGAEUS Gently, gently, go easy, beetle; don't start off so proudly, or trust at first too greatly to your powers; wait till you have sweated, till the beating of your wings shall make your limb joints supple. Above all things, don't let off some foul smell, I adjure you; else I would rather have you stop in the stable altogether.

SECOND SERVANT Poor master! Is he crazy?

TRYGAEUS Silence! silence!

SECOND SERVANT (TO TRYGAEUS) But why start up into the air on chance?

TRYGAEUS 'Tis for the weal of all the Greeks; I am attempting a daring and novel feat.

SECOND SERVANT But what is your purpose? What useless folly!

TRYGAEUS No words of ill omen! Give vent to joy and command all men to keep silence, to close down their drains and privies with new tiles and to stop up their own vent-holes.(1)

f(1) Fearing that if it caught a whiff from earth to its

liking, the beetle might descend from the highest heaven to

satisfy itself.

FIRST SERVANT No, I shall not be silent, unless you tell me where you are going.

TRYGAEUS Why, where am I likely to be going across the sky, if it be not to visit Zeus?

FIRST SERVANT For what purpose?

TRYGAEUS I want to ask him what he reckons to do for all the Greeks.

SECOND SERVANT And if he doesn't tell you?

TRYGAEUS I shall pursue him at law as a traitor who sells Greece to the Medes.(1)

f(1) The Persians and the Spartans were not then allied as

the scholiast states, since a treaty between them was only

concluded in 412 B.C., i.e. eight years after the production of 'Peace'; the great king, however, was trying to derive

advantages out of the dissensions in Greece.

SECOND SERVANT Death seize me, if I let you go.

TRYGAEUS It is absolutely necessary.

SECOND SERVANT Alas! alas! dear little girls, your father is deserting you secretly to go to heaven. Ah! poor orphans, entreat him, beseech him.

LITTLE DAUGHTER Father! father! what is this I hear? Is it true? What! you would leave me, you would vanish into the sky, you would go to the crows?(1) 'Tis impossible! Answer, father, an you love me.

f(1) "Go to the crows," a proverbial expression equivalent

to our "Go to the devil."

TRYGAEUS Yes, I am going. You hurt me too sorely, my daughters, when you ask me for bread, calling me your daddy, and there is not the ghost of an obolus in the house; if I succeed and come back, you will have a barley loaf every morning—and a punch in the eye for sauce!

LITTLE DAUGHTER But how will you make the journey? 'Tis not a ship that will carry you thither.

TRYGAEUS No, but this winged steed will.

LITTLE DAUGHTER But what an idea, daddy, to harness a beetle, on which to fly to the gods.

TRYGAEUS We see from Aesop's fables that they alone can fly to the abode of the Immortals.(1)

f(1) Aesop tells us that the eagle and the beetle were at

war; the eagle devoured the beetle's young and the latter

got into its nest and tumbled out its eggs. On this the

eagle complained to Zeus, who advised it to lay its eggs in

his bosom; but the beetle flew up to the abode of Zeus, who,

forgetful of the eagle's eggs, at once rose to chase off the

objectionable insect. The eggs fell to earth and were

smashed to bits.

LITTLE DAUGHTER Father, father, 'tis a tale nobody can believe! that such a stinking creature can have gone to the gods.

TRYGAEUS It went to have vengeance on the eagle and break its eggs.

LITTLE DAUGHTER Why not saddle Pegasus? you would have a more TRAGIC(1) appearance in the eyes of the gods.

f(1) Pegasus is introduced by Euripides both in his

'Andromeda' and his 'Bellerophon.'

TRYGAEUS Eh! don't you see, little fool, that then twice the food would be wanted? Whereas my beetle devours again as filth what I have eaten myself.

LITTLE DAUGHTER And if it fell into the watery depths of the sea, could it escape with its wings?

TRYGAEUS (EXPOSING HIMSELF) I am fitted with a rudder in case of need, and my Naxos beetle will serve me as a boat.(1)

f(1) Boats, called 'beetles,' doubtless because in form they

resembled these insects, were built at Naxos.

LITTLE DAUGHTER And what harbour will you put in at?

TRYGAEUS Why is there not the harbour of Cantharos at the Piraeus?(1)

f(1) Nature had divided the Piraeus into three basins—

Cantharos, Aphrodisium and Zea. (Cantharos) is Greek for

dung-beetle.

LITTLE DAUGHTER Take care not to knock against anything and so fall off into space; once a cripple, you would be a fit subject for Euripides, who would put you into a tragedy.(1)

f(1) In allusion to Euripides' fondness for introducing lame

heroes in his plays.

TRYGAEUS I'll see to it. Good-bye! (TO THE ATHENIANS.) You, for love of whom I brave these dangers, do ye neither let wind nor go to stool for the space of three days, for, if, while cleaving the air, my steed should scent anything, he would fling me head foremost from the summit of my hopes. Now come, my Pegasus, get a-going with up-pricked ears and make your golden bridle resound gaily. Eh! what are you doing? What are you up to? Do you turn your nose towards the cesspools? Come, pluck up a spirit; rush upwards from the earth, stretch out your speedy wings and make straight for the palace of Zeus; for once give up foraging in your daily food.—Hi! you down there, what are you after now? Oh! my god! 'tis a man emptying his belly in the Piraeus, close to the house where the bad girls are. But is it my death you seek then, my death? Will you not bury that right away and pile a great heap of earth upon it and plant wild thyme therein and pour perfumes on it? If I were to fall from up here and misfortune happened to me, the town of Chios(1) would owe a fine of five talents for my death, all along of your cursed rump. Alas! how frightened I am! oh! I have no heart for jests. Ah! machinist, take great care of me. There is already a wind whirling round my navel; take great care or, from sheer fright, I shall form food for my beetle.... But I think I am no longer far from the gods; aye, that

---

is the dwelling of Zeus, I perceive. Hullo! Hi! where is the doorkeeper? Will
no one open?

f(1) An allusion to the proverbial nickname applied to the

Chians (in Greek)—'crapping Chian.' There is a further

joke, of course, in connection with the hundred and one

frivolous pretexts which the Athenians invented for exacting

contributions from the maritime allies.

(THE SCENE CHANGES AND HEAVEN IS PRESENTED.)

HERMES Meseems I can sniff a man. (HE PERCEIVES TRYGAEUS ASTRIDE HIS BEETLE.) Why, what plague is this?

TRYGAEUS A horse-beetle.

HERMES Oh! impudent, shameless rascal! oh! scoundrel! triple scoundrel! the greatest scoundrel in the world! how did you come here? Oh! scoundrel of all scoundrels! your name? Reply.

TRYGAEUS Triple scoundrel.

HERMES Your country?

TRYGAEUS Triple scoundrel.

HERMES Your father?

TRYGAEUS My father? Triple scoundrel.

HERMES By the Earth, you shall die, unless you tell me your name.

TRYGAEUS I am Trygaeus of the Athmonian deme, a good vine-dresser, little addicted to quibbling and not at all an informer.

HERMES Why do you come?

TRYGAEUS I come to bring you this meat.

HERMES Ah! my good friend, did you have a good journey?

TRYGAEUS Glutton, be off! I no longer seem a triple scoundrel to you. Come, call Zeus.

HERMES Ah! ah! you are a long way yet from reaching the gods, for they moved yesterday.

TRYGAEUS To what part of the earth?

HERMES Eh! of the earth, did you say?

TRYGAEUS In short, where are they then?

HERMES Very far, very far, right at the furthest end of the dome of heaven.

TRYGAEUS But why have they left you all alone here?

HERMES I am watching what remains of the furniture, the little pots and pans, the bits of chairs and tables, and odd wine-jars.

TRYGAEUS And why have the gods moved away?

HERMES Because of their wrath against the Greeks. They have located War in the house they occupied themselves and have given him full power to do with you exactly as he pleases; then they went as high up as ever they could, so as to see no more of your fights and to hear no more of your prayers.

TRYGAEUS What reason have they for treating us so?

HERMES Because they have afforded you an opportunity for peace more than once, but you have always preferred war. If the Laconians got the very slightest advantage, they would exclaim, "By the Twin Brethren! the Athenians shall smart for this." If, on the contrary, the latter triumphed and the Laconians came with peace proposals, you would say, "By Demeter, they want to deceive us. No, by Zeus, we will not hear a word; they will always be coming as long as we hold Pylos."(1)

f(1) Masters of Pylos and Sphacteria, the Athenians had

brought home the three hundred prisoners taken in the latter

place in 425 B.C.; the Spartans had several times sent

envoys to offer peace and to demand back both Pylos and the

prisoners, but the Athenian pride had caused these proposals to be long refused. Finally the prisoners had been given up

in 423 B.C., but the War was continued nevertheless.

TRYGAEUS Yes, that is quite the style our folk do talk in.

HERMES So that I don't know whether you will ever see Peace again.

TRYGAEUS Why, where has she gone to then?

HERMES War has cast her into a deep pit.

TRYGAEUS Where?

HERMES Down there, at the very bottom. And you see what heaps of stones he has piled over the top, so that you should never pull her out again.

TRYGAEUS Tell me, what is War preparing against us?

HERMES All I know is that last evening he brought along a huge mortar.

TRYGAEUS And what is he going to do with his mortar?

HERMES He wants to pound up all the cities of Greece in it.... But I must say good-bye, for I think he is coming out; what an uproar he is making!

TRYGAEUS Ah! great gods! let us seek safety; meseems I already hear the noise of this fearful war mortar.

WAR (ENTERS, CARRYING A HUGE MORTAR) Oh! mortals, mortals, wretched mortals, how your jaws will snap!

TRYGAEUS Oh! divine Apollo! what a prodigious big mortar! Oh, what misery the very sight of War causes me! This then is the foe from whom I fly, who is so cruel, so formidable, so stalwart, so solid on his legs!

WAR Oh! Prasiae!(1) thrice wretched, five times, aye, a thousand times wretched! for thou shalt be destroyed this day.

f(1) An important town in Eastern Laconia on the Argolic

gulf, celebrated for a temple where a festival was held

annually in honour of Achilles. It had been taken and

pillaged by the Athenians in the second year of the

Peloponnesian War, 430 B.C. As he utters this imprecation,

War throws some leeks, the root-word of the name Praisae,

into his mortar.

TRYGAEUS This does not concern us over much; 'tis only so much the worse for the Laconians.

WAR Oh! Megara! Megara! how utterly are you going to be ground up! what fine mincemeat(1) are you to be made into!

f(1) War throws some garlic into his mortar as emblematical

of the city of Megara, where it was grown in abundance.

TRYGAEUS Alas! alas! what bitter tears there will be among the Megarians!(1)

f(1) Because the smell of bruised garlic causes the eyes to

water.

WAR Oh, Sicily! you too must perish! Your wretched towns shall be grated like this cheese.(1) Now let us pour some Attic honey(2) into the mortar.

f(1) He throws cheese into the mortar as emblematical of

Sicily, on account of its rich pastures.

f(2) Emblematical of Athens. They honey of Mount Hymettus

was famous.

TRYGAEUS Oh! I beseech you! use some other honey; this kind is worth four obols; be careful, oh! be careful of our Attic honey.

WAR Hi! Tumult, you slave there!

TUMULT What do you want?

WAR Out upon you! Standing there with folded arms! Take this cuff o' the head for your pains.

TUMULT Oh! how it stings! Master, have you got garlic in your fist, I wonder?

WAR Run and fetch me a pestle.

TUMULT But we haven't got one; 'twas only yesterday we moved.

WAR Go and fetch me one from Athens, and hurry, hurry!

TUMULT Aye, I hasten there; if I return without one, I shall have no cause for laughing. (EXIT.)

TRYGAEUS Ah! what is to become of us, wretched mortals that we are? See the danger that threatens if he returns with the pestle, for War will quietly amuse himself with pounding all the towns of Hellas to pieces. Ah! Bacchus! cause this herald of evil to perish on his road!

WAR Well?

TUMULT (WHO HAS RETURNED) Well, what?

WAR You have brought back nothing?

TUMULT Alas! the Athenians have lost their pestle—the tanner, who ground Greece to powder.(1)

f(1) Cleon, who had lately fallen before Amphipolis, in 422

B.C.

TRYGAEUS Oh! Athene, venerable mistress! 'tis well for our city he is dead, and before he could serve us with this hash.

WAR Then go and seek one at Sparta and have done with it!

TUMULT Aye, aye, master!

WAR Be back as quick as ever you can.

TRYGAEUS (TO THE AUDIENCE) What is going to happen, friends? 'Tis the critical hour. Ah! if there is some initiate of Samothrace(1) among you, 'tis surely the moment to wish this messenger some accident—some sprain or strain.

f(1) An island in the Aegean Sea, on the coast of Thrace and

opposite the mouth of the Hebrus; the Mysteries are said to

have found their first home in this island, where the

Cabirian gods were worshipped; this cult, shrouded in deep

mystery to even the initiates themselves, has remained an

almost insoluble problem for the modern critic. It was said

that the wishes of the initiates were always granted, and

they were feared as to-day the 'jettatori' (spell-throwers,

casters of the evil eye) in Sicily are feared.

19

TUMULT (WHO RETURNS) Alas! alas! thrice again, alas!

WAR What is it? Again you come back without it?

TUMULT The Spartans too have lost their pestle.

WAR How, varlet?

TUMULT They had lent it to their allies in Thrace,(1) who have lost it for them.

f(1) Brasidas perished in Thrace in the same battle as Cleon

   at Amphipolis, 422 B.C.

TRYGAEUS Long life to you, Thracians! My hopes revive, pluck up courage, mortals!

WAR Take all this stuff away; I am going in to make a pestle for myself.

TRYGAEUS 'Tis now the time to sing as Datis did, as he abused himself at high noon, "Oh pleasure! oh enjoyment! oh delights!" 'Tis now, oh Greeks! the moment when freed of quarrels and fighting, we should rescue sweet Peace and draw her out of this pit, before some other pestle prevents us. Come, labourers, merchants, workmen, artisans, strangers, whether you be domiciled or not, islanders, come here, Greeks of all countries, come hurrying here with picks and levers and ropes! 'Tis the moment to drain a cup in honour of the Good Genius.

CHORUS Come hither all! quick, hasten to the rescue! All peoples of Greece, now is the time or never, for you to help each other. You see yourselves freed from battles and all their horrors of bloodshed. The day, hateful to Lamachus(1), has come. Come then, what must be done? Give your orders, direct us, for I swear to work this day without ceasing, until with the help of our levers and our engines we have drawn back into light the greatest of all goddesses, her to whom the olive is so dear.

f(1) An Athenian general as ambitious as he was brave. In

423 B.C. he had failed in an enterprise against Heracles, a

storm having destroyed his fleet. Since then he had

distingued himself in several actions, and was destined,

some years later, to share the command of the expedition to

Sicily with Alcibiades and Nicias.

TRYGAEUS Silence! if War should hear your shouts of joy he would bound forth from his retreat in fury.

CHORUS Such a decree overwhelms us with joy; how different to the edict, which bade us muster with provisions for three days.(1)

f(1) Meaning, to start a military expedition.

TRYGAEUS Let us beware lest the cursed Cerberus(1) prevent us even from the nethermost hell from delivering the goddess by his furious howling, just as he did when on earth.

f(1) Cleon.

CHORUS Once we have hold of her, none in the world will be able to take her from us. Huzza! huzza!(1)

f(1) The Chorus insist on the conventional choric dance.

TRYGAEUS You will work my death if you don't subdue your shouts. War will come running out and trample everything beneath his feet.

CHORUS Well then! LET him confound, let him trample, let him overturn everything! We cannot help giving vent to our joy.

TRYGAEUS Oh! cruel fate! My friends! in the name of the gods, what possesses you? Your dancing will wreck the success of a fine undertaking.

CHORUS 'Tis not I who want to dance; 'tis my legs that bound with delight.

TRYGAEUS Enough, an you love me, cease your gambols.

CHORUS There! 'Tis over.

TRYGAEUS You say so, and nevertheless you go on.

CHORUS Yet one more figure and 'tis done.

TRYGAEUS Well, just this one; then you must dance no more.

CHORUS No, no more dancing, if we can help you.

TRYGAEUS But look, you are not stopping even now.

CHORUS By Zeus, I am only throwing up my right leg, that's all.

TRYGAEUS Come, I grant you that, but pray, annoy me no further.

CHORUS Ah! the left leg too will have its fling; well, 'tis but its right. I am so happy, so delighted at not having to carry my buckler any more. I sing and I laugh more than if I had cast my old age, as a serpent does its skin.

TRYGAEUS No, 'tis not time for joy yet, for you are not sure of success. But when you have got the goddess, then rejoice, shout and laugh; thenceforward you will be able to sail or stay at home, to make love or sleep, to attend festivals and processions, to play at cottabos,(1) live like true Sybarites and to shout, Io, io!

f(1) One of the most favourite games with the Greeks. A

stick was set upright in the ground and to this the beam of

a balance was attached by its centre. Two vessels were hung from the extremities of the beam so as to balance; beneath

these two other and larger dishes were placed and filled

with water, and in the middle of each a brazen figure,

called Manes, was stood. The game consisted in throwing

drops of wine from an agreed distance into one or the other

vessel, so that, dragged downwards by the weight of the

liquor, it bumped against Manes.

CHORUS Ah! God grant we may see the blessed day. I have suffered so much; have so oft slept with Phormio(1) on hard beds. You will no longer find me an acid, angry, hard judge as heretofore, but will find me turned indulgent and grown younger by twenty years through happiness. We have been killing ourselves long enough, tiring ourselves out with going to the Lyceum(2) and returning laden with spear and buckler.—But what can we do to please you? Come, speak; for 'tis a good Fate that has named you our leader.

f(1) A general of austere habits; he disposed of all his

property to pay the cost of a naval expedition, in which he

beat the fleet of the foe off the promontory of Rhium in 429

B.C.

f(2) The Lyceum was a portico ornamented with paintings and

surrounded with gardens, in which military exercises took

place.

TRYGAEUS How shall we set about removing these stones?

HERMES Rash reprobate, what do you propose doing?

TRYGAEUS Nothing bad, as Cillicon said.(1)

f(1) A citizen of Miletus, who betrayed his country to the

people of Pirene. When asked what he purposed, he replied,

"Nothing bad," which expression had therefore passed into a

proverb.

HERMES You are undone, you wretch.

TRYGAEUS Yes, if the lot had to decide my life, for Hermes would know how to turn the chance.(1)

f(1) Hermes was the god of chance.

HERMES You are lost, you are dead.

TRYGAEUS On what day?

HERMES This instant.

TRYGAEUS But I have not provided myself with flour and cheese yet(1) to start for death.

f(1) As the soldiers had to do when starting on an

expedition.

HERMES You ARE kneaded and ground already, I tell you.(1)

f(1) That is, you are predicated.

TRYGAEUS Hah! I have not yet tasted that gentle pleasure.

HERMES Don't you know that Zeus has decreed death for him who is surprised exhuming Peace?

TRYGAEUS What! must I really and truly die?

HERMES You must.

TRYGAEUS Well then, lend me three drachmae to buy a young pig; I wish to have myself initiated before I die.(1)

f(1) The initiated were thought to enjoy greater happiness

after death.

HERMES Oh! Zeus, the Thunderer!(1)

f(1) He summons Zeus to reveal Trygaeus' conspiracy.

TRYGAEUS I adjure you in the name of the gods, master, don't denounce us!

HERMES I may not, I cannot keep silent.

TRYGAEUS In the name of the meats which I brought you so good-naturedly.

HERMES Why, wretched man, Zeus will annihilate me, if I do not shout out at the top of my voice, to inform him what you are plotting.

TRYGAEUS Oh, no! don't shout, I beg you, dear little Hermes.... And what are you doing, comrades? You stand there as though you were stocks and stones. Wretched men, speak, entreat him at once; otherwise he will be shouting.

CHORUS Oh! mighty Hermes! don't do it; no, don't do it! If ever you have eaten some young pig, sacrificed by us on your altars, with pleasure, may this offering not be without value in your sight to-day.

TRYGAEUS Do you not hear them wheedling you, mighty god?

CHORUS Be not pitiless toward our prayers; permit us to deliver the goddess. Oh! the most human, the most generous of the gods, be favourable toward us, if it be true that you detest the haughty crests and proud brows of Pisander;(1) we shall never cease, oh master, offering you sacred victims and solemn prayers.

f(1) An Athenian captain who later had the recall of

Alcibiades decreed by the Athenian people; in 'The Birds'

Aristophanes represents him as a cowardly beggar. He was

the reactionary leader who established the Oligarchical

Government of the Four Hundred, 411 B.C., after the failure

of the Syracusan expedition.

TRYGAEUS Have mercy, mercy, let yourself be touched by their words; never was your worship so dear to them as to-day.

HERMES I' truth, never have you been greater thieves.(1)

f(1) Among other attributes, Hermes was the god of thieves.

TRYGAEUS I will reveal a great, a terrible conspiracy against the gods to you.

HERMES Hah! speak and perchance I shall let myself be softened.

TRYGAEUS Know then, that the Moon and that infamous Sun are plotting against you, and want to deliver Greece into the hands of the Barbarians.

HERMES What for?

TRYGAEUS Because it is to you that we sacrifice, whereas the barbarians worship them; hence they would like to see you destroyed, that they alone might receive the offerings.

HERMES 'Tis then for this reason that these untrustworthy charioteers have for so long been defrauding us, one of them robbing us of daylight and the other nibbling away at the other's disk.(1)

f(1) Alluding to the eclipses of the sun and the moon.

TRYGAEUS Yes, certainly. So therefore, Hermes, my friend, help us with your whole heart to find and deliver the captive and we will celebrate the great Panathenaea(1) in your honour as well as all the festivals of the other gods; for Hermes shall be the Mysteries, the Dipolia, the Adonia; everywhere the towns, freed from their miseries, will sacrifice to Hermes the Liberator; you will be loaded with benefits of every kind, and to start with, I offer you this cup for libations as your first present.

f(1) The Panathenaea were dedicated to Athene, the Mysteries

to Demeter, the Dipolia to Zeus, the Adonia to Aphrodite and

Adonis. Trygaeus promises Hermes that he shall be worshipped

in the place of the other gods.

HERMES Ah! how golden cups do influence me! Come, friends, get to work. To the pit quickly, pick in hand, and drag away the stones.

CHORUS We go, but you, cleverest of all the gods, supervise our labours; tell us, good workman as you are, what we must do; we shall obey your orders with alacrity.

TRYGAEUS Quick, reach me your cup, and let us preface our work by addressing prayers to the gods.

HERMES Oh! sacred, sacred libations! Keep silence, oh! ye people! keep silence!

TRYGAEUS Let us offer our libations and our prayers, so that this day may begin an era of unalloyed happiness for Greece and that he who has bravely pulled at the rope with us may never resume his buckler.

CHORUS Aye, may we pass our lives in peace, caressing our mistresses and poking the fire.

TRYGAEUS May he who would prefer the war, oh Dionysus, be ever drawing barbed arrows out of his elbows.

HERMES If there be a citizen, greedy for military rank and honours who refuses, oh, divine Peace! to restore you to daylight, may he behave as cowardly as Cleonymus on the battlefield.

TRYGAEUS If a lance-maker or a dealer in shields desires war for the sake of better trade, may he be taken by pirates and eat nothing but barley.

CHORUS If some ambitious man does not help us, because he wants to become a General, or if a slave is plotting to pass over to the enemy, let his limbs be broken on the wheel, may he be beaten to death with rods! As for us, may Fortune favour us! Io! Paean, Io!

TRYGAEUS Don't say Paean,(1) but simply, Io.

f(1) The pun here cannot be kept. The word (in Greek),

Paean, resembles (that for) to strike; hence the word, as

recalling the blows and wounds of the war, seems of ill omen

to Trygaeus.

HERMES Very well, then! Io! Io! I'll simply say, Io!

TRYGAEUS To Hermes, the Graces, Hora, Aphrodite, Eros!

28

CHORUS But not to Ares?

TRYGAEUS No.

CHORUS Nor doubtless to Enyalius?

TRYGAEUS No.

CHORUS Come, all strain at the ropes to tear away the stones. Pull!

HERMES Heave away, heave, heave, oh!

CHORUS Come, pull harder, harder.

HERMES Heave away, heave, heave, oh!

CHORUS Still harder, harder still.

HERMES Heave away, heave! Heave away, heave, heave, oh!

TRYGAEUS Come, come, there is no working together. Come! all pull at the same instant! you Boeotians are only pretending. Beware!

HERMES Come, heave away, heave!

CHORUS Hi! you two pull as well.

TRYGAEUS Why, I am pulling, I am hanging on to the rope and straining till I am almost off my feet; I am working with all my might.

CHORUS Why does not the work advance then?

TRYGAEUS Lamachus, this is too bad! You are in the way, sitting there. We have no use for your Medusa's head, friend.(1)

f(1) The device on his shield was a Gorgon's head. (See

'The Acharnians.')

HERMES But hold, the Argives have not pulled the least bit; they have done nothing but laugh at us for our pains while they were getting gain with both hands.(1)

f(1) Both Sparta and Athens had sought the alliance of the

Argives; they had kept themselves strictly neutral and had

received pay from both sides. But, the year after the

production of 'The Wasps,' they openly joined Athens, had

attacked Epidaurus and got cut to pieces by the Spartans.

TRYGAEUS Ah! my dear sir, the Laconians at all events pull with vigour.

CHORUS But look! only those among them who generally hold the plough-tail show any zeal,(1) while the armourers impede them in their efforts.

f(1) These are the Spartan prisoners from Sphacteria, who

were lying in goal at Athens. They were chained fast to

large beams of wood.

HERMES And the Megarians too are doing nothing, yet look how they are pulling and showing their teeth like famished curs; The poor wretches are dying of hunger!(1)

f(1) 'Twas want of force, not want of will. They had

suffered more than any other people from the war. (See 'The

Acharnians.')

TRYGAEUS This won't do, friends. Come! all together! Everyone to the work and with a good heart for the business.

HERMES Heave away, heave!

TRYGAEUS Harder!

HERMES Heave away, heave!

TRYGAEUS Come on then, by heaven.

HERMES Heave away, heave! Heave away, heave!

CHORUS This will never do.

TRYGAEUS Is it not a shame? some pull one way and others another. You, Argives there, beware of a thrashing!

HERMES Come, put your strength into it.

TRYGAEUS Heave away, heave!

CHORUS There are many ill-disposed folk among us.

TRYGAEUS Do you at least, who long for peace, pull heartily.

CHORUS But there are some who prevent us.

HERMES Off to the Devil with you, Megarians! The goddess hates you. She recollects that you were the first to rub her the wrong way. Athenians, you are not well placed for pulling. There you are too busy with law-suits; if you really want to free the goddess, get down a little towards the sea.(1)

f(1) Meaning, look chiefly to your fleet. This was the

counsel that Themistocles frequently gave the Athenians.

CHORUS Come, friends, none but husbandmen on the rope.

HERMES Ah! that will do ever so much better.

CHORUS He says the thing is going well. Come, all of you, together and with a will.

TRYGAEUS 'Tis the husbandmen who are doing all the work.

CHORUS Come then, come, and all together! Hah! hah! at last there is some unanimity in the work. Don't let us give up, let us redouble our efforts. There! now we have it! Come then, all together! Heave away, heave! Heave away, heave! Heave away, heave! Heave away, heave! Heave away, heave! All together! (PEACE IS DRAWN OUT OF THE PIT.)

TRYGAEUS Oh! venerated goddess, who givest us our grapes, where am I to find the ten-thousand-gallon words(1) wherewith to greet thee? I have none such at home. Oh! hail to thee, Opora,(2) and thee, Theoria!(3) How beautiful is thy face! How sweet thy breath! What gentle fragrance comes from thy bosom, gentle as freedom from military duty, as the most dainty perfumes!

f(1) A metaphor referring to the abundant vintages that

peace would assure.

f(2) The goddess of fruits.

f(3) Aristophanes personifies under this name the sacred

ceremonies in general which peace would allow to be

celebrated with due pomp. Opora and Theoria come on the

stage in the wake of Peace, clothed and decked out as

courtesans.

HERMES Is it then a smell like a soldier's knapsack?

TRYGAEUS Oh! hateful soldier! your hideous satchel makes me sick! it stinks like the belching of onions, whereas this lovable deity has the odour of sweet fruits, of festivals, of the Dionysia, of the harmony of flutes, of the comic poets, of the verses of Sophocles, of the phrases of Euripides...

HERMES That's a foul calumny, you wretch! She detests that framer of subtleties and quibbles.

TRYGAEUS ...of ivy, of straining-bags for wine, of bleating ewes, of provision-laden women hastening to the kitchen, of the tipsy servant wench, of the upturned wine-jar, and of a whole heap of other good things.

HERMES Then look how the reconciled towns chat pleasantly together, how they laugh; and yet they are all cruelly mishandled; their wounds are bleeding still.

TRYGAEUS But let us also scan the mien of the spectators; we shall thus find out the trade of each.

HERMES Ah! good gods! Look at that poor crest-maker, tearing at his hair,(1) and at that pike-maker, who has just broken wind in yon sword-cutler's face.

f(1) Aristophanes has already shown us the husbandmen and

workers in peaceful trades pulling at the rope the extricate

Peace, while the armourers hindered them by pulling the

other way.

TRYGAEUS And do you see with what pleasure this sickle-maker is making long noses at the spear-maker?

HERMES Now ask the husbandmen to be off.

TRYGAEUS Listen, good folk! Let the husbandmen take their farming tools and return to their fields as quick as possible, but without either sword, spear or javelin. All is as quiet as if Peace had been reigning for a century. Come, let everyone go till the earth, singing the Paean.

CHORUS Oh, thou, whom men of standing desired and who art good to husbandmen, I have gazed upon thee with delight; and now I go to greet my vines, to caress after so long an absence the fig trees I planted in my youth.

TRYGAEUS Friends, let us first adore the goddess, who has delivered us from crests and Gorgons;(1) then let us hurry to our farms, having first bought a nice little piece of salt fish to eat in the fields.

f(1) An allusion to Lamachus' shield.

HERMES By Posidon! what a fine crew they make and dense as the crust of a cake; they are as nimble as guests on their way to a feast.

TRYGAEUS See, how their iron spades glitter and how beautifully their three-pronged mattocks glisten in the sun! How regularly they align the plants! I also burn myself to go into the country and to turn over the earth I have so long neglected.—Friends, do you remember the happy life that Peace afforded us formerly; can you recall the splendid baskets of figs, both fresh and dried, the myrtles, the sweet wine, the violets blooming near the spring, and the olives, for which we have wept so much? Worship, adore the goddess for restoring you so many blessings.

CHORUS Hail! hail! thou beloved divinity! thy return overwhelms us with joy. When far from thee, my ardent wish to see my fields again made me pine with regret. From thee came all blessings. Oh! much desired Peace! thou art the sole support of those who spend their lives tilling the earth. Under thy rule we had a thousand delicious enjoyments at our beck; thou wert the husbandman's wheaten cake and his safeguard. So that our vineyards, our young fig-tree woods and all our plantations hail thee with delight and smile at thy coming. But where was she then, I wonder, all the long time she spent away from us? Hermes, thou benevolent god, tell us!

HERMES Wise husbandmen, hearken to my words, if you want to know why she was lost to you. The start of our misfortunes was the exile of Phidias;(1) Pericles feared he might share his ill-luck, he mistrusted your peevish nature and, to prevent all danger to himself, he threw out that little spark, the Megarian decree,(2) set the city aflame, and blew up the conflagration with a hurricane of war, so that the smoke drew tears from all Greeks both here and over there. At the very outset of this fire our vines were a-crackle, our casks knocked together;(3) it was beyond the power of any man to stop the disaster, and Peace disappeared.

f(1) Having been commissioned to execute a statue of Athene,

Phidias was accused of having stolen part of the gold given

him out of the public treasury for its decoration. Rewarded

for his work by calumny and banishment, he resolved to make

a finer statue than his Athene, and executed one for the

temple of Elis, that of the Olympian Zeus, which was

considered one of the wonders of the world.

f(2) He had issued a decree, which forbade the admission of

any Megarian on Attic soil, and also all trade with that

people. The Megarians, who obtained all their provisions

from Athens, were thus almost reduced to starvation.

f(3) That is, the vineyards were ravaged from the very

outset of the war, and this increased the animosity.

TRYGAEUS That, by Apollo! is what no one ever told me; I could not think what connection there could be between Phidias and Peace.

CHORUS Nor I; I know it now. This accounts for her beauty, if she is related to him. There are so many things that escape us.

HERMES Then, when the towns subject to you saw that you were angered one against the other and were showing each other your teeth like dogs, they hatched a thousand plots to pay you no more dues and gained over the chief citizens of Sparta at the price of gold. They, being as shamelessly greedy as they were faithless in diplomacy, chased off Peace with ignominy to let loose War. Though this was profitable to them, 'twas the ruin of the husbandmen, who were innocent of all blame; for, in revenge, your galleys went out to devour their figs.

TRYGAEUS And 'twas with justice too; did they not break down my black fig tree, which I had planted and dunged with my own hands?

CHORUS Yes, by Zeus! yes, 'twas well done; the wretches broke a chest for me with stones, which held six medimni of corn.

HERMES Then the rural labourers flocked into the city(1) and let themselves be bought over like the others. Not having even a grape-stone to munch and longing after their figs, they looked towards the orators.(2) These well knew that the poor were driven to extremity and lacked even bread; but they nevertheless drove away the Goddess, each time she reappeared in answer to the wish of the country, with their loud shrieks that were as sharp as pitchforks; furthermore, they attacked the well-filled purses of the richest among our allies on the pretence that they belonged to Brasidas' party.(3) And then you would tear the poor accused wretch to pieces with your teeth; for the city, all pale with hunger and cowed with terror, gladly snapped up any calumny that was thrown it to devour. So the strangers, seeing what terrible blows the informers dealt, sealed their lips with gold. They grew rich, while you, alas! you could only see that Greece was going to ruin. 'Twas the tanner who was the author of all this woe.(4)

f(1) Driven in from the country parts by the Lacedaemonian

invaders.

f(2) The demagogues, who distributed the slender dole given

to the poor, and by that means exercised undue power over

them.

f(3) Meaning, the side of the Spartans.

f(4) Cleon.

TRYGAEUS Enough said, Hermes, leave that man in Hades, whither he has gone; he no longer belongs to us, but rather to yourself.(1) That he was a cheat, a braggart, a calumniator when alive, why, nothing could be truer; but anything you might say now would be an insult to one of your own folk. Oh! venerated Goddess! why art thou silent?

f(1) It was Hermes who conducted the souls of the dead down

to the lower regions.

HERMES And how could she speak to the spectators? She is too angry at all that they have made her suffer.

TRYGAEUS At least let her speak a little to you, Hermes.

HERMES Tell me, my dear, what are your feelings with regard to them? Come, you relentless foe of all bucklers, speak; I am listening to you. (PEACE WHISPERS INTO HERMES' EAR.) Is that your grievance against them? Yes, yes, I understand. Hearken, you folk, this is her complaint. She says, that after the affair of Pylos(1) she came to you unbidden to bring you a basket full of truces and that you thrice repulsed her by your votes in the assembly.

f(1) The Spartans had thrice offered to make peace after the

Pylos disaster.

TRYGAEUS Yes, we did wrong, but forgive us, for our mind was then entirely absorbed in leather.(1)

f(1) i.e. dominated by Cleon.

HERMES Listen again to what she has just asked me. Who was her greatest foe here? and furthermore, had she a friend who exerted himself to put an end to the fighting?

TRYGAEUS Her most devoted friend was Cleonymus; it is undisputed.

HERMES How then did Cleonymus behave in fights?

TRYGAEUS Oh! the bravest of warriors! Only he was not born of the father he claims; he showed it quick enough in the army by throwing away his weapons.(1)

f(1) There is a pun here that cannot be rendered between

(the Greek for) 'one who throws away his weapons' and 'a

supposititious child.'

HERMES There is yet another question she has just put to me. Who rules now in the rostrum?

38

TRYGAEUS 'Tis Hyperbolus, who now holds empire on the Pnyx. (TO PEACE) What now? you turn away your head!

HERMES She is vexed, that the people should give themselves a wretch of that kind for their chief.

TRYGAEUS Oh! we shall not employ him again; but the people, seeing themselves without a leader, took him haphazard, just as a man, who is naked, springs upon the first cloak he sees.

HERMES She asks, what will be the result of such a choice of the city?

TRYGAEUS We shall be more far-seeing in consequence.

HERMES And why?

TRYGAEUS Because he is a lamp-maker. Formerly we only directed our business by groping in the dark; now we shall only deliberate by lamplight.

HERMES Oh! oh! what questions she does order me to put to you!

TRYGAEUS What are they?

HERMES She wants to have news of a whole heap of old-fashioned things she left here. First of all, how is Sophocles?

TRYGAEUS Very well, but something very strange has happened to him.

HERMES What then?

TRYGAEUS He has turned from Sophocles into Simonides.(1)

f(1) Simonides was very avaricious, and sold his pen to the

highest bidder. It seems that Sophocles had also started

writing for gain.

HERMES Into Simonides? How so?

39

TRYGAEUS Because, though old and broken-down as he is, he would put to sea on a hurdle to gain an obolus.(1)

f(1) i.e. he would recoil from no risk to turn an honest

penny.

HERMES And wise Cratinus,(1) is he still alive?

f(1) A comic poet as well known for his love of wine as for

his writings; he died in 431 B.C., the first year of the

war, at the age of ninety-seven.

TRYGAEUS He died about the time of the Laconian invasion.

HERMES How?

TRYGAEUS Of a swoon. He could not bear the shock of seeing one of his casks full of wine broken. Ah! what a number of other misfortunes our city has suffered! So, dearest mistress, nothing can now separate us from thee.

HERMES If that be so, receive Opora here for a wife; take her to the country, live with her, and grow fine grapes together.(1)

f(1) Opora was the goddess of fruits.

TRYGAEUS Come, my dear friend, come and accept my kisses. Tell me, Hermes, my master, do you think it would hurt me to love her a little, after so long an abstinence?

HERMES No, not if you swallow a potion of penny-royal afterwards.(1) But hasten to lead Theoria(2) to the Senate; 'twas there she lodged before.

f(1) The scholiast says fruit may be eaten with impunity in

great quantities if care is taken to drink a decoction of

this herb afterwards.

f(2) Theoria is confided to the care of the Senate, because

it was this body who named the deputies appointed to go and

consult the oracles beyond the Attic borders to be present

at feats and games.

TRYGAEUS Oh! fortunate Senate! Thanks to Theoria, what soups you will swallow for the space of three days!(1) how you will devour meats and cooked tripe! Come, farewell, friend Hermes!

f(1) The great festivals, e.g. the Dionysia, lasted three

days. Those in honour of the return of Peace, which was so

much desired, could not last a shorter time.

HERMES And to you also, my dear sir, may you have much happiness, and don't forget me.

TRYGAEUS Come, beetle, home, home, and let us fly on a swift wing.

HERMES Oh! he is no longer here.

TRYGAEUS Where has he gone to then?

HERMES He is harnessed to the chariot of Zeus and bears the thunder bolts.

TRYGAEUS But where will the poor wretch get his food?

HERMES He will eat Ganymede's ambrosia.

TRYGAEUS Very well then, but how am I going to descend?

HERMES Oh! never fear, there is nothing simpler; place yourself beside the goddess.

TRYGAEUS Come, my pretty maidens, follow me quickly; there are plenty of folk awaiting you with ready weapons.

CHORUS Farewell and good luck be yours! Let us begin by handing over all this gear to the care of our servants, for no place is less safe than a theatre; there is always a crowd of thieves prowling around it, seeking to find some mischief to do. Come, keep a good watch over all this. As for ourselves, let us explain to the spectators what we have in our minds, the purpose of our play.

Undoubtedly the comic poet who mounted the stage to praise himself in the parabasis would deserve to be handed over to the sticks of the beadles. Nevertheless, oh Muse, if it be right to esteem the most honest and illustrious of our comic writers at his proper value, permit our poet to say that he thinks he has deserved a glorious renown. First of all, 'tis he who has compelled his rivals no longer to scoff at rags or to war with lice; and as for those Heracles, always chewing and ever hungry, those poltroons and cheats who allow themselves to be beaten at will, he was the first to cover them with ridicule and to chase them from the stage;(1) he has also dismissed that slave, whom one never failed to set a-weeping before you, so that his comrade might have the chance of jeering at his stripes and might ask, "Wretch, what has happened to your hide? Has the lash rained an army of its thongs on you and laid your back waste?" After having delivered us from all these wearisome ineptitudes and these low buffooneries, he has built up for us a great art, like a palace with high towers, constructed of fine phrases, great thoughts and of jokes not common on the streets. Moreover 'tis not obscure private persons or women that he stages in his comedies; but, bold as Heracles, 'tis the very greatest whom he attacks, undeterred by the fetid stink of leather or the threats of hearts of mud. He has the right to say, "I am the first ever dared to go straight for that beast with the sharp teeth and the terrible eyes that flashed lambent fire like those of Cynna,(2) surrounded by a hundred lewd flatterers, who spittle-licked him to his heart's content; it had a voice like a roaring torrent, the stench of a seal, a foul Lamia's testicles and the rump of a camel."(3)

I did not recoil in horror at the sight of such a monster, but fought him relentlessly to win your deliverance and that of the Islanders. Such are the services which should be graven in your recollection and entitle me to your thanks. Yet I have not been seen frequenting the wrestling school intoxicated with success and trying to tamper with young boys;(4) but I took all my theatrical gear(5) and returned straight home. I pained folk but little and caused them much amusement; my conscience rebuked me for nothing. Hence both grown men and youths should be on my side and I likewise invite the bald(6) to give me their votes; for, if I triumph, everyone will say, both at table and at festivals, "Carry this to the bald man, give these cakes to the bald one, do not grudge the poet whose talent shines as bright as his own bare skull the share he deserves."

Oh, Muse! drive the War far from our city and come to preside over our dances, if you love me; come and celebrate the nuptials of the gods, the banquets of us mortals and the festivals of the fortunate; these are the themes that inspire thy most poetic songs. And should Carcinus come to beg thee for admission with his sons to thy chorus, refuse all traffic with them; remember they are but gelded birds, stork-necked dancers, mannikins about as tall as a pat of goat dung, in fact machine-made poets.(7) Contrary to all expectation, the father has at last managed to finish a piece, but he owns himself that a cat strangled it one fine evening.(8)

Such are the songs(9) with which the Muse with the glorious hair inspires the able poet and which enchant the assembled populace, when the spring swallow twitters beneath the foliage;(10) but the god spare us from the chorus of Morsimus and that of Melanthius!(11) Oh! what a bitter discordancy grated upon my ears that day when the tragic chorus was directed by this same Melanthius and his brother, these two Gorgons,(12) these two harpies, the plague of the seas, whose gluttonous bellies devour the entire race of fishes, these followers of old women, these goats with their stinking arm-pits. Oh! Muse, spit upon them abundantly and keep the feast gaily with me.

f(1) In spite of what he says, Aristophanes has not always

disdained this sort of low comedy—for instance, his

Heracles in 'The Birds.'

f(2) A celebrated Athenian courtesan of Aristophanes' day.

f(3) Cleon. These four verses are here repeated from the

parabasis of 'The Wasps,' produced 423 B.C., the year before

this play.

f(4) Shafts aimed at certain poets, who used their renown as

a means of seducing young men to grant them pederastic

favours.

f(5) The poet supplied everything needful for the production

of his piece—vases, dresses, masks, etc.

f(6) Aristophanes was bald himself, it would seem.

f(7) Carcinus and his three sons were both poets and dancers. (See the closing scene of 'The Wasps.') Perhaps relying little on the literary value of their work, it seems that they sought to please the people by the magnificence of its staging.

f(8) He had written a piece called 'The Mice,' which he succeeded with great difficulty in getting played, but it met with no success.

f(9) This passage really follows on the invocation, "Oh, Muse! drive the War," etc., from which indeed it is only divided by the interpolated criticism aimed at Carcinus.

f(10) The scholiast informs us that these verses are borrowed from a poet of the sixth century B.C.

f(11) Sons of Philocles, of the family of Aeschylus, tragic writers, derided by Aristophanes as bad poets and notorious gluttons.

f(12) The Gorgons were represented with great teeth, and therefore the same name was given to gluttons. The Harpies, to whom the two voracious poets are also compared, were monsters with the face of a woman, the body of a vulture and hooked beak and claws.

TRYGAEUS Ah! 'tis a rough job getting to the gods! my legs are as good as broken through it. How small you were, to be sure, when seen from heaven! you had all the appearance too of being great rascals; but seen close, you look even worse.

SERVANT Is that you, master?

TRYGAEUS So I've been told.

SERVANT What has happened to you?

TRYGAEUS My legs pain me; it is such a plaguey long journey.

SERVANT Oh! tell me...

TRYGAEUS What?

SERVANT Did you see any other man besides yourself strolling about in heaven?

TRYGAEUS No, only the souls of two or three dithyrambic poets.

SERVANT What were they doing up there?

TRYGAEUS They were seeking to catch some lyric exordia as they flew by immersed in the billows of the air.

SERVANT Is it true, what they tell us, that men are turned into stars after death?

TRYGAEUS Quite true.

SERVANT Then who is that star I see over yonder?

TRYGAEUS That is Ion of Chios,(1) the author of an ode beginning "Morning"; as soon as ever he got to heaven, they called him "the Morning Star."

f(1) A tragic and dithyrambic poet, who had written many

pieces, which had met with great success at Athens.

SERVANT And those stars like sparks, that plough up the air as they dart across the sky?(1)

f(1) The shooting stars.

TRYGAEUS They are the rich leaving the feast with a lantern and a light inside it.—But hurry up, show this young girl into my house, clean out the bath, heat some water and prepare the nuptial couch for herself and me. When 'tis done, come back here; meanwhile I am off to present this one to the Senate.

SERVANT But where then did you get these pretty chattels?

TRYGAEUS Where? why in heaven.

SERVANT I would not give more than an obolus for gods who have got to keeping brothels like us mere mortals.

TRYGAEUS They are not all so, but there are some up there too who live by this trade.

SERVANT Come, that's rich! But I bethink me, shall I give her something to eat?

TRYGAEUS No, for she would neither touch bread nor cake; she is used to licking ambrosia at the table of the gods.

SERVANT Well, we can give her something to lick down here too.

CHORUS Here is a truly happy old man, as far as I can judge.

TRYGAEUS Ah! but what shall I be, when you see me presently dressed for the wedding?

48

CHORUS Made young again by love and scented with perfumes, your lot will be one we all shall envy.

TRYGAEUS And when I lie beside her and caress her bosoms?

CHORUS Oh! then you will be happier than those spinning-tops who call Carcinus their father.(1)

f(1) It has already been mentioned that the sons of Carcinus

were dancers.

TRYGAEUS And I well deserve it; have I not bestridden a beetle to save the Greeks, who now, thanks to me, can make love at their ease and sleep peacefully on their farms?

SERVANT The girl has quitted the bath; she is charming from head to foot, both belly and buttocks; the cake is baked and they are kneading the sesame-biscuit;(1) nothing is lacking but the bridegroom's virility.

f(1) It was customary at weddings, says Menander, to give

the bride a sesame-caked as an emblem of fruitfulness,

because sesame is the most fruitful of all seeds.

TRYGAEUS Let us first hasten to lodge Theoria in the hands of the Senate.

SERVANT But tell me, who is this woman?

TRYGAEUS Why, 'tis Theoria, with whom we used formerly to go to Brauron,(1) to get tipsy and frolic. I had the greatest trouble to get hold of her.

f(1) An Attic town on the east coast, noted for a

magnificent temple, in which stood the statue of Artemis,

---

which Orestes and Iphigenia had brought from the Tauric

Chersonese and also for the Brauronia, festivals that were

celebrated every four years in honour of the goddess. This

was one of the festivals which the Attic people kept with

the greatest pomp, and was an occasion for debauchery.

SERVANT Ah! you charmer! what pleasure your pretty bottom will afford me every four years!

TRYGAEUS Let us see, who of you is steady enough to be trusted by the Senate with the care of this charming wench? Hi! you, friend! what are you drawing there?

SERVANT I am drawing the plan of the tent I wish to erect for myself on the isthmus.(1)

f(1) Competitors intending to take part in the great

Olympic, Isthmian and other games took with them a tent,

wherein to camp in the open. Further, there is an obscene

allusion which the actor indicates by a gesture.

TRYGAEUS Come, who wishes to take the charge of her? No one? Come, Theoria, I am going to lead you into the midst of the spectators and confide you to their care.

SERVANT Ah! there is one who makes a sign to you.

TRYGAEUS Who is it?

SERVANT 'Tis Ariphrades. He wishes to take her home at once.

TRYGAEUS No, I'm sure he shan't. He would soon have her done for, absorbing all her life-force. Come, Theoria, put down all this gear.(1)

Senate, Prytanes, look upon Theoria and see what precious blessings I place in your hands. Hasten to raise its limbs and to immolate the victim. Admire the fine chimney,(2) it is quite black with smoke, for 'twas here that the Senate did their cooking before the war. Now that you have found Theoria again, you can start the most charming games from to-morrow, wrestling with her on the ground, either on your hands and feet, or you can lay her on her side, or stand before her with bent knees, or, well rubbed with oil, you can boldly enter the lists, as in the Pancratium, belabouring your foe with blows from your fist or otherwise. The next day you will celebrate equestrian games, in which the riders will ride side by side, or else the chariot teams, thrown one on top of another, panting and whinnying, will roll and knock against each other on the ground, while other rivals, thrown out of their seats, will fall before reaching the goal, utterly exhausted by their efforts.—Come, Prytanes, take Theoria. Oh! look how graciously yonder fellow has received her; you would not have been in such a hurry to introduce her to the Senate, if nothing were coming to you through it;(3) you would not have failed to plead some holiday as an excuse.

f(1) Doubtless the vessels and other sacrificial objects and

implements with which Theoria was laden in her character of

presiding deity at religious ceremonies.

f(2) Where the meats were cooked after sacrifice; this also

marks the secondary obscene sense he means to convey.

f(3) One of the offices of the Prytanes was to introduce

those who asked admission to the Senate, but it would seem

that none could obtain this favour without payment. Without

this, a thousand excuses would be made; for instance, it

would be a public holiday, and consequently the Senate could

receive no one. As there was some festival nearly every

day, he whose purse would not open might have to wait a very

long while.

CHORUS Such a man as you assures the happiness of all his fellow-citizens.

TRYGAEUS When you are gathering your vintages you will prize me even better.

CHORUS E'en from to-day we hail you as the deliverer of mankind.

TRYGAEUS Wait until you have drunk a beaker of new wine, before you appraise my true merits.

CHORUS Excepting the gods, there is none greater than yourself, and that will ever be our opinion.

TRYGAEUS Yea, Trygaeus of Athmonia has deserved well of you, he has freed both husbandman and craftsman from the most cruel ills; he has vanquished Hyberbolus.

SERVANT Well then, what must be done now?

TRYGAEUS You must offer pots of green-stuff to the goddess to consecrate her altars.

SERVANT Pots of green-stuff(1) as we do to poor Hermes—and even he thinks the fare but mean?

f(1) This was only offered to lesser deities.

TRYGAEUS What will you offer them? A fatted bull?

SERVANT Oh no! I don't want to start bellowing the battle-cry.(1)

f(1) In the Greek we have a play upon the similarity of the

words (for) a bull, and to shout the battle-cry.

TRYGAEUS A great fat swine then?

SERVANT No, no.

TRYGAEUS Why not?

SERVANT We don't want any of the swinishness of Theagenes.(1)

f(1) Theagenes, of the Piraeus, a hideous, coarse, debauched

and evil-living character of the day.

TRYGAEUS What other victim do you prefer then?

SERVANT A sheep.

TRYGAEUS A sheep?

SERVANT Yes.

TRYGAEUS But you must give the word the Ionic form.

SERVANT Purposely. So that if anyone in the assembly says, "We must go to war," all may start bleating in alarm, "Oi, oi."(1)

f(1) That is the vocative of the Ionic form of the word; in

Attic Greek it is contracted throughout.

TRYGAEUS A brilliant idea.

SERVANT And we shall all be lambs one toward the other, yea, and milder still toward the allies.

TRYGAEUS Then go for the sheep and haste to bring it back with you; I will prepare the altar for the sacrifice.

CHORUS How everything succeeds to our wish, when the gods are willing and Fortune favours us! how opportunely everything falls out.

TRYGAEUS Nothing could be truer, for look! here stands the altar all ready at my door.

CHORUS Hurry, hurry, for the winds are fickle; make haste, while the divine will is set on stopping this cruel war and is showering on us the most striking benefits.

TRYGAEUS Here is the basket of barley-seed mingled with salt, the chaplet and the sacred knife; and there is the fire; so we are only waiting for the sheep.

CHORUS Hasten, hasten, for, if Chaeris sees you, he will come without bidding, he and his flute; and when you see him puffing and panting and out of breath, you will have to give him something.

TRYGAEUS Come, seize the basket and take the lustral water and hurry to circle round the altar to the right.

SERVANT There! 'tis done. What is your next bidding?

TRYGAEUS Hold! I take this fire-brand first and plunge it into the water.

SERVANT Be quick! be quick! Sprinkle the altar.

TRYGAEUS Give me some barley-seed, purify yourself and hand me the basin; then scatter the rest of the barley among the audience.

SERVANT 'Tis done.

TRYGAEUS You have thrown it?

SERVANT Yes, by Hermes! and all the spectators have had their share.

TRYGAEUS But not the women?

SERVANT Oh! their husbands will give it them this evening.(1)

f(1) An obscene jest.

TRYGAEUS Let us pray! Who is here? Are there any good men?(1)

f(1) Before sacrificing, the officiating person asked, "Who

is here?" and those present answered, "Many good men."

SERVANT Come, give, so that I may sprinkle these. Faith! they are indeed good, brave men.

TRYGAEUS You believe so?

SERVANT I am sure, and the proof of it is that we have flooded them with lustral water and they have not budged an inch.(1)

f(1) The actors forming the chorus are meant here.

TRYGAEUS Come, then, to prayers; to prayers, quick!—Oh! Peace, mighty queen, venerated goddess, thou, who presidest over choruses and at nuptials, deign to accept the sacrifices we offer thee.

SERVANT Receive it, greatly honoured mistress, and behave not like the coquettes, who half open the door to entice the gallants, draw back when they are stared at, to return once more if a man passes on. But do not act like this to us.

TRYGAEUS No, but like an honest woman, show thyself to thy worshippers, who are worn with regretting thee all these thirteen years. Hush the noise of battle, be a true Lysimacha to us.(1) Put an end to this tittle-tattle, to this idle babble, that set us defying one another. Cause the Greeks once more to taste the pleasant beverage of friendship and temper all hearts with the gentle feeling of forgiveness. Make excellent commodities flow to our markets, fine heads of garlic, early cucumbers, apples, pomegranates and nice little cloaks for the slaves; make them bring geese, ducks, pigeons and larks from Boeotia and baskets of eels from Lake Copais; we shall all rush to buy them, disputing their possession with Morychus, Teleas, Glaucetes and every other glutton. Melanthius(2) will arrive on the market last of all; 'twill be, "no more eels, all sold!" and then he'll start a-groaning and exclaiming as in his monologue of Medea,(3) "I am dying, I am dying! Alas! I have let those hidden in the beet escape me!"(4) And won't we laugh? These are the wishes, mighty goddess, which we pray thee to grant.

f(1) Lysimacha is derived from (the Greek for) put an end

to, and (the Greek for) fight.

f(2) A tragic poet, reputed a great gourmand.

f(3) A tragedy by Melanthius.

f(4) Eels were cooked with beet.—A parody on some verses in

the 'Medea' of Melanthius.

SERVANT Take the knife and slaughter the sheep like a finished cook.

TRYGAEUS No, the goddess does not wish it.(1)

f(1) As a matter of fact, the Sicyonians, who celebrated the

festival of Peace on the sixteenth day of the month of

Hecatombeon (July), spilled no blood upon her altar.

SERVANT And why not?

TRYGAEUS Blood cannot please Peace, so let us spill none upon her altar. Therefore go and sacrifice the sheep in the house, cut off the legs and bring them here; thus the carcase will be saved for the choregus.

CHORUS You, who remain here, get chopped wood and everything needed for the sacrifice ready.

TRYGAEUS Don't I look like a diviner preparing his mystic fire?

CHORUS Undoubtedly. Will anything that it behooves a wise man to know escape you? Don't you know all that a man should know, who is distinguished for his wisdom and inventive daring?

TRYGAEUS There! the wood catches. Its smoke blinds poor Stilbides.(1) I am now going to bring the table and thus be my own slave.

f(1) A celebrated diviner, who had accompanied the Athenians

on their expedition to Sicily. Thus the War was necessary

to make his calling pay and the smoke of the sacrifice

offered to Peace must therefore be unpleasant to him.

CHORUS You have braved a thousand dangers to save your sacred town. All honour to you! your glory will be ever envied.

SERVANT Hold! Here are the legs, place them upon the altar. For myself, I mean to go back to the entrails and the cakes.

TRYGAEUS I'll see to those; I want you here.

SERVANT Well then, here I am. Do you think I have been long?

TRYGAEUS Just get this roasted. Ah! who is this man, crowned with laurel, who is coming to me?

SERVANT He has a self-important look; is he some diviner?

TRYGAEUS No, I' faith! 'tis Hierocles.

SERVANT Ah! that oracle-monger from Oreus.(1) What is he going to tell us?

f(1) A town in Euboea on the channel which separated that

island from Thessaly.

TRYGAEUS Evidently he is coming to oppose the peace.

SERVANT No, 'tis the odour of the fat that attracts him.

TRYGAEUS Let us appear not to see him.

SERVANT Very well.

HIEROCLES What sacrifice is this? to what god are you offering it?

TRYGAEUS (TO THE SERVANT) Silence!—(ALOUD.) Look after the roasting and keep your hands off the meat.

HIEROCLES To whom are you sacrificing? Answer me. Ah! the tail(1) is showing favourable omens.

f(1) When sacrificing, the tail was cut off the victim and thrown into the fire. From the way in which it burnt the

inference was drawn as to whether or not the sacrifice was

agreeable to the deity.

SERVANT Aye, very favourable, oh, loved and mighty Peace!

HIEROCLES Come, cut off the first offering(1) and make the oblation.

f(1) This was the part that belonged to the priests and

diviners. As one of the latter class, Hierocles is in haste

to see this piece cut off.

TRYGAEUS 'Tis not roasted enough.

HIEROCLES Yea, truly, 'tis done to a turn.

TRYGAEUS Mind your own business, friend! (TO THE SERVANT.) Cut away. Where is the table? Bring the libations.

HIEROCLES The tongue is cut separately.

TRYGAEUS We know all that. But just listen to one piece of advice.

HIEROCLES And that is?

TRYGAEUS Don't talk, for 'tis divine Peace to whom we are sacrificing.

HIEROCLES Oh! wretched mortals, oh, you idiots!

TRYGAEUS Keep such ugly terms for yourself.

HIEROCLES What! you are so ignorant you don't understand the will of the gods and you make a treaty, you, who are men, with apes, who are full of malice?(1)

59

f(1) The Spartans.

TRYGAEUS Ha, ha, ha!

HIEROCLES What are you laughing at?

TRYGAEUS Ha, ha! your apes amuse me!

HIEROCLES You simple pigeons, you trust yourselves to foxes, who are all craft, both in mind and heart.

TRYGAEUS Oh, you trouble-maker! may your lungs get as hot as this meat!

HIEROCLES Nay, nay! if only the Nymphs had not fooled Bacis, and Bacis mortal men; and if the Nymphs had not tricked Bacis a second time...(1)

f(1) Emphatic pathos, incomprehensible even to the diviner

himself; this is a satire on the obscure style of the

oracles. Bacis was a famous Boeotian diviner.

TRYGAEUS May the plague seize you, if you don't stop wearying us with your Bacis!

HIEROCLES ...it would not have been written in the book of Fate that the bends of Peace must be broken; but first...

TRYGAEUS The meat must be dusted with salt.

HIEROCLES ...it does not please the blessed gods that we should stop the War until the wolf uniteth with the sheep.

TRYGAEUS How, you cursed animal, could the wolf ever unite with the sheep?

HIEROCLES As long as the wood-bug gives off a fetid odour, when it flies; as long as the noisy bitch is forced by nature to litter blind pups, so long shall peace be forbidden.

TRYGAEUS Then what should be done? Not to stop War would be to leave it to the decision of chance which of the two people should suffer the most, whereas by uniting under a treaty, we share the empire of Greece.

HIEROCLES You will never make the crab walk straight.

TRYGAEUS You shall no longer be fed at the Prytaneum; the war done, oracles are not wanted.

HIEROCLES You will never smooth the rough spikes of the hedgehog.

TRYGAEUS Will you never stop fooling the Athenians?

HIEROCLES What oracle ordered you to burn these joints of mutton in honour of the gods?

TRYGAEUS This grand oracle of Homer's: "Thus vanished the dark war-clouds and we offered a sacrifice to new-born Peace. When the flame had consumed the thighs of the victim and its inwards had appeased our hunger, we poured out the libations of wine." 'Twas I who arranged the sacred rites, but none offered the shining cup to the diviner.(1)

f(1) Of course this is not a bona fide quotation, but a

whimsical adaptation of various Homeric verses; the last is

a coinage of his own, and means, that he is to have no part,

either in the flesh of the victim or in the wine of the

libations.

HIEROCLES I care little for that. 'Tis not the Sibyl who spoke it.(1)

f(1) Probably the Sibyl of Delphi is meant.

TRYGAEUS Wise Homer has also said: "He who delights in the horrors of civil war has neither country nor laws nor home." What noble words!

HIEROCLES Beware lest the kite turn your brain and rob...

TRYGAEUS Look out, slave! This oracle threatens our meat. Quick, pour the libation, and give me some of the inwards.

HIEROCLES I too will help myself to a bit, if you like.

TRYGAEUS The libation! the libation!

HIEROCLES Pour out also for me and give me some of this meat.

TRYGAEUS No, the blessed gods won't allow it yet; let us drink; and as for you, get you gone, for 'tis their will. Mighty Peace! stay ever in our midst.

HIEROCLES Bring the tongue hither.

TRYGAEUS Relieve us of your own.

HIEROCLES The libation.

TRYGAEUS Here! and this into the bargain (STRIKES HIM).

HIEROCLES You will not give me any meat?

TRYGAEUS We cannot give you any until the wolf unites with the sheep.

HIEROCLES I will embrace your knees.

TRYGAEUS 'Tis lost labour, good fellow; you will never smooth the rough spikes of the hedgehog.... Come, spectators, join us in our feast.

HIEROCLES And what am I to do?

TRYGAEUS You? go and eat the Sibyl.

HIEROCLES No, by the Earth! no, you shall not eat without me; if you do not give, I take; 'tis common property.

TRYGAEUS (TO THE SERVANT) Strike, strike this Bacis, this humbugging soothsayer.

HIEROCLES I take to witness...

TRYGAEUS And I also, that you are a glutton and an impostor. Hold him tight and beat the impostor with a stick.

SERVANT You look to that; I will snatch the skin from him which he has stolen from us.(1) Are you going to let go that skin, you priest from hell! do you hear! Oh! what a fine crow has come from Oreus! Stretch your wings quickly for Elymnium.(2)

f(1) The skin of the victim, that is to say.

f(2) A temple in Euboea, close to Oreus. The servant means,

"Return where you came from."

CHORUS Oh! joy, joy! no more helmet, no more cheese nor onions!(1) No, I have no passion for battles; what I love, is to drink with good comrades in the corner by the fire when good dry wood, cut in the height of the summer, is crackling; it is to cook pease on the coals and beechnuts among the embers, 'tis to kiss our pretty Thracian(2) while my wife is at the bath. Nothing is more pleasing, when the rain is sprouting our sowings, than to chat with some friend, saying, "Tell me, Comarchides, what shall we do? I would willingly drink myself, while the heavens are watering our fields. Come, wife, cook three measures of beans, adding to them a little wheat, and give us some figs. Syra! call Manes off the fields, 'tis impossible to prune the vine or to align the ridges, for the ground is too wet to-day. Let someone bring me the thrush and those two chaffinches; there were also some curds and four pieces of hare, unless the cat stole them last evening, for I know not what the infernal noise was that I heard in the house. Serve up three of the pieces for me, slave, and give the fourth to my father. Go and ask Aeschinades for some myrtle branches with berries on them, and then, for 'tis the same road, you will invite Charinades to come and drink with me to the honour of the gods who watch over our crops." When the grasshopper sings his dulcet tune, I love to see the Lemnian vines beginning to ripen, for 'tis the earliest plant of all. I love likewise to watch the fig filling out, and when it has reached maturity I eat with appreciation and exclaim, "Oh! delightful season!" Then too I bruise some thyme and infuse it in water. Indeed I grow a great deal fatter passing the summer in this way than in watching a cursed captain with his three plumes and his military cloak of a startling crimson (he calls it true Sardian purple), which he takes care to dye himself with Cyzicus saffron in a battle; then he is the first to run away, shaking his plumes like a great yellow prancing cock,(3) while I am left to watch the nets.(4) Once back again in Athens, these brave fellows behave abominably; they write down these, they scratch through others, and this backwards and forwards two or three times at random. The departure is set for to-morrow, and some citizen has brought no provisions, because he didn't know he had to go; he stops in front of the statue of Pandion,(5) reads his name, is dumbfounded and starts away at a run, weeping bitter tears. The townsfolk are less ill-used, but that is how the husbandmen are treated by these men of war, the hated of the gods and of men, who know nothing but how to throw away their shield. For this reason, if it please heaven, I propose to call these rascals to account, for they are lions in times of peace, but sneaking foxes when it comes to fighting.

f(1) This was the soldier's usual ration on duty.

f(2) Slaves often bore the name of the country of their

birth.

f(3) Because of the new colour which fear had lent his

chlamys.

f(4) Meaning, that he deserts his men in mid-campaign,

leaving them to look after the enemy.

f(5) Ancient King of Athens. This was one of the twelve

statues, on the pedestals of which the names of the soldiers

chose for departure on service were written. The decrees

were also placarded on them.

TRYGAEUS Oh! oh! what a crowd for the nuptial feast! Here! dust the tables with this crest, which is good for nothing else now. Halloa! produce the cakes, the thrushes, plenty of good jugged hare and the little loaves.

A SICKLE-MAKER Trygaeus, where is Trygaeus?

TRYGAEUS I am cooking the thrushes.

SICKLE-MAKER Trygaeus, my best of friends, what a fine stroke of business you have done for me by bringing back Peace! Formerly my sickles would not have sold at an obolus apiece; to-day I am being paid fifty drachmae for every one. And here is a neighbour who is selling his casks for the country at three drachmae each. So come, Trygaeus, take as many sickles and casks as you will for nothing. Accept them for nothing; 'tis because of our handsome profits on our sales that we offer you these wedding presents.

TRYGAEUS Thanks. Put them all down inside there, and come along quick to the banquet. Ah! do you see that armourer yonder coming with a wry face?

A CREST-MAKER Alas! alas! Trygaeus, you have ruined me utterly.

TRYGAEUS What! won't the crests go any more, friend?

CREST-MAKER You have killed my business, my livelihood, and that of this poor lance-maker too.

TRYGAEUS Come, come, what are you asking for these two crests?

CREST-MAKER What do you bid for them?

TRYGAEUS What do I bid? Oh! I am ashamed to say. Still, as the clasp is of good workmanship, I would give two, even three measures of dried figs; I could use 'em for dusting the table.

CREST-MAKER All right, tell them to bring me the dried figs; 'tis always better than nothing.

TRYGAEUS Take them away, be off with your crests and get you gone; they are moulting, they are losing all their hair; I would not give a single fig for them.

A BREASTPLATE-MAKER Good gods, what am I going to do with this fine ten-minae breastplate, which is so splendidly made?

TRYGAEUS Oh, you will lose nothing over it.

BREASTPLATE-MAKER I will sell it to you at cost price.

TRYGAEUS 'Twould be very useful as a night-stool...

BREASTPLATE-MAKER Cease your insults, both to me and my wares.

TRYGAEUS ...if propped on three stones. Look, 'tis admirable.

BREASTPLATE-MAKER But how can you wipe, idiot?

TRYGAEUS I can pass one hand through here, and the other there, and so...

BREASTPLATE-MAKER What! do you wipe with both hands?

TRYGAEUS Aye, so that I may not be accused of robbing the State, by blocking up an oar-hole in the galley.(1)

f(1) The trierarchs stopped up some of the holes made for

the oars, in order to reduce the number of rowers they had

to supply for the galleys; they thus saved the wages of the

rowers they dispensed with.

BREASTPLATE-MAKER So you would pay ten minae(1) for a night-stool?

f(1) The mina was equivalent to about three pounds, ten

shillings.

TRYGAEUS Undoubtedly, you rascal. Do you think I would sell my rump for a thousand drachmae?(1)

f(1) Which is the same thing, since a mina was worth a

hundred drachmae.

BREASTPLATE-MAKER Come, have the money paid over to me.

TRYGAEUS No, friend; I find it hurts me to sit on. Take it away, I won't buy it.

A TRUMPET-MAKER What is to be done with this trumpet, for which I gave sixty drachmae the other day?

TRYGAEUS Pour lead into the hollow and fit a good, long stick to the top; and you will have a balanced cottabos.(1)

f(1) For 'cottabos' see note above.

TRUMPET-MAKER Ha! would you mock me?

TRYGAEUS Well, here's another notion. Pour in lead as I said, add here a dish hung on strings, and you will have a balance for weighing the figs which you give your slaves in the fields.

A HELMET-MAKER Cursed fate! I am ruined. Here are helmets, for which I gave a mina each. What I to do with them? who will buy them?

TRYGAEUS Go and sell them to the Egyptians; they will do for measuring loosening medicines.(1)

f(1) Syrmoea, a kind of purgative syrup much used by the

Egyptians, made of antiscorbutic herbs, such as mustard,

horse-radish, etc.

A SPEAR-MAKER Ah! poor helmet-maker, things are indeed in a bad way.

TRYGAEUS That man has no cause for complaint.

SPEAR-MAKER But helmets will be no more used.

TRYGAEUS Let him learn to fit a handle to them and he can sell them for more money.(1)

f(1) As wine-pots or similar vessels.

SPEAR-MAKER Let us be off, comrade.

TRYGAEUS No, I want to buy these spears.

SPEAR-MAKER What will you give?

TRYGAEUS If they could be split in two, I would take them at a drachma per hundred to use as vine-props.

SPEAR-MAKER The insolent dog! Let us go, friend.

TRYGAEUS Ah! here come the guests, children from the table to relieve themselves; I fancy they also want to hum over what they will be singing presently. Hi! child! what do you reckon to sing? Stand there and give me the opening line.

THE SON OF LAMACHUS "Glory to the young warriors..."

TRYGAEUS Oh! leave off about your young warriors, you little wretch; we are at peace and you are an idiot and a rascal.

SON OF LAMACHUS "The skirmish begins, the hollow bucklers clash against each other."(1)

  f(1) These verses and those which both Trygaeus and the son

  of Lamachus quote afterwards are borrowed from the 'Iliad.'

TRYGAEUS Bucklers! Leave me in peace with your bucklers.

SON OF LAMACHUS "And then there came groanings and shouts of victory."

TRYGAEUS Groanings! ah! by Bacchus! look out for yourself, you cursed squaller, if you start wearying us again with your groanings and hollow bucklers.

SON OF LAMACHUS Then what should I sing? Tell me what pleases you.

TRYGAEUS "'Tis thus they feasted on the flesh of oxen," or something similar, as, for instance, "Everything that could tickle the palate was placed on the table."

SON OF LAMACHUS "'Tis thus they feasted on the flesh of oxen and, tired of warfare, unharnessed their foaming steeds."

TRYGAEUS That's splendid; tired of warfare, they seat themselves at table; sing, sing to us how they still go on eating after they are satiated.

SON OF LAMACHUS "The meal over, they girded themselves..."

TRYGAEUS With good wine, no doubt?

SON OF LAMACHUS "...with armour and rushed forth from the towers, and a terrible shout arose."

TRYGAEUS Get you gone, you little scapegrace, you and your battles! You sing of nothing but warfare. Who is your father then?

SON OF LAMACHUS My father?

TRYGAEUS Why yes, your father.

SON OF LAMACHUS I am Lamachus' son.

TRYGAEUS Oh! oh! I could indeed have sworn, when I was listening to you, that you were the son of some warrior who dreams of nothing but wounds and bruises, of some Boulomachus or Clausimachus;(1) go and sing your plaguey songs to the spearmen.... Where is the son of Cleonymus? Sing me something before going back to the feast. I am at least certain he will not sing of battles, for his father is far too careful a man.

f(1) Boulomachus is derived from (two Greek words meaning)

to wish for battle; Clausimachus from (two others), the

tears that battles cost. The same root (for) 'battle' is

also contained in the name Lamachus.

SON OF CLEONYMUS "An inhabitant of Sais is parading with the spotless shield which I regret to say I have thrown into a thicket."(1)

f(1) A distich borrowed from Archilochus, a celebrated poet

of the seventh century B.C., born at Paros, and the author

of odes, satires, epigrams and elegies. He sang his own

shame. 'Twas in an expedition against Sais, not the town in

Egypt as the similarity in name might lead one to believe,

but in Thrace, that he had cast away his buckler. "A might

calamity truly!" he says without shame. "I shall buy

another."

TRYGAEUS Tell me, you little good-for-nothing, are you singing that for your father?

SON OF CLEONYMUS "But I saved my life."

TRYGAEUS And dishonoured your family. But let us go in; I am very certain, that being the son of such a father, you will never forget this song of the buckler. You, who remain to the feast, 'tis your duty to devour dish after dish and not to ply empty jaws. Come, put heart into the work and eat with your mouths full. For, believe me, poor friends, white teeth are useless furniture, if they chew nothing.

CHORUS Never fear; thanks all the same for your good advice.

TRYGAEUS You, who yesterday were dying of hunger, come, stuff yourselves with this fine hare-stew; 'tis not every day that we find cakes lying neglected. Eat, eat, or I predict you will soon regret it.

CHORUS Silence! Keep silence! Here is the bride about to appear! Take nuptial torches and let all rejoice and join in our songs. Then, when we have danced, clinked our cups and thrown Hyperbolus through the doorway we will carry back all our farming tools to the fields and shall pray the gods to give wealth to the Greeks and to cause us all to gather in an abundant barley harvest, enjoy a noble vintage, to grant that we may choke with good figs, that our wives may prove fruitful, that in fact we may recover all our lost blessings, and that the sparkling fire may be restored to the hearth.

TRYGAEUS Come, wife, to the fields and seek, my beauty, to brighten and enliven my nights. Oh! Hymen! oh! Hymenaeus!

CHORUS Oh! Hymen! oh! Hymenaeus! oh! thrice happy man, who so well deserve your good fortune!

TRYGAEUS Oh! Hymen! oh! Hymenaeus!

CHORUS Oh! Hymen! oh! Hymenaeus!

FIRST SEMI-CHORUS What shall we do to her?

SECOND SEMI-CHORUS What shall we do to her?

FIRST SEMI-CHORUS We will gather her kisses.

SECOND SEMI-CHORUS We will gather her kisses.

CHORUS Come, comrades, we who are in the first row, let us pick up the bridegroom and carry him in triumph. Oh! Hymen! oh! Hymenaeus! Oh! Hymen! oh! Hymenaeus!

TRYGAEUS Oh! Hymen! oh! Hymenaeus!

CHORUS You shall have a fine house, no cares and the finest of figs. Oh! Hymen! oh! Hymenaeus!

TRYGAEUS Oh! Hymen! oh! Hymenaeus!

CHORUS The bridegroom's fig is great and thick; the bride's very soft and tender.

TRYGAEUS While eating and drinking deep draughts of wine, continue to repeat: Oh! Hymen! oh! Hymenaeus!

CHORUS Oh! Hymen! oh! Hymenaeus!

TRYGAEUS Farewell, farewell, my friends. All who come with me shall have cakes galore.

The End